Copyright © 2020 All she is.
All rights reserved. No part of this publication may be reproduced, distributed, or transmitted in any form or by any means, including photocopying, recording, or other electronic or mechanical methods, without the prior written permission of the publisher, except in the case of brief quotations embodied in critical reviews and certain other noncommercial uses permitted by copyright law. For permission requests, write to the publisher, addressed "Attention: Permissions Coordinator," at the e-mail address below.

davina@alegriamagazine.com

ISBN: 978-1-7347252-8-5
Published by Alegria publishing

All she is

A BILINGUAL POETRY COLLECTION

Cynthia J. Villa

Para Mi Mami,

Que tu luz continue guiando mi camino.

Maria Lourdes Villa Ramírez
1967 – 2004

Foreword

I met Villa in a soccer field of a working-class neighborhood in Los Angeles County where our families came together on the weekends. These weekends brought a sense of joy, rest, and normalcy to a community of mostly immigrant families bridging their past and their present. She was a player and I was on the sidelines cheerleading her and the rest of the team. Since then, I've been a fan of this fierce woman, now embarking on this exciting project; a project that is an invitation to All she is and much more. It is an invitation to feel the pain, the joy, the grief, the love; and to experience the ways that words can transcend one person, the ways they can go beyond imagined borders and hopefully leave a mark on the reader. Whether this mark is validation, inspiration, or simple pleasure, I hope that you reflect on, and maybe even discover some, if not many parts of you as you turn each page. In engaging with this work you are also supporting the mission that a range of storytellers, observations, and perspectives be nourish. This is no trivial mission as it is being carried out in a shifting socio-political context in which those who have held power and influence are being challenged but are not giving up this power without a fight. Storytellers, poets, and all other cultural workers are an important voice in this fight; a fight worth cheerleading on.

Diana Y. Cardenas, LCSW

Preface

Poetry, for me, began as a way of coping with my mother's death. I was fourteen years old, and I had so much to say yet, I had no one to tell it to. In silence and with a pen and paper, I mourned her. In poetry form and open letters, I learned to express all the emptiness I felt. For many years I believed I was destined to be broken. And so, I continued writing, convincing myself that every word would put myself back together. I was wrong. It took me fifteen years to realize I was more than just my dead mother's missing voice. And so, I began creating my own.

I have never considered myself a Poet. I never dared to give myself such a description. As a minority member, I grew up thinking that people who are like me, Mexican American, brown-skinned girl, who lived in Mexico for four years and *solo aprendió hablar en Español*. A girl born with all the citizenship rights but who could not masticate the *gringo's idioma*, so I took ESL classes *cuando regrese al Norte in 2000*. A girl whose fourth-grade teacher, who was also of Mexican descent, told me I wouldn't amount anything in life but be a janitor for not knowing the multiplication table of eleven (*en Michoacán solo me instruyeron hasta el diez*). A woman who now casually and accidentally blurs an accent when she speaks. A woman who, at times in the middle of a conversation, runs out of words because she cannot articulate her ideas or a woman who can't remember the name of *frutas en inglés* but knows them all in Spanish; usually don't amount to such a title.

For many years, I kept my art private. It was intimate. I was selfish. It was only mine to be. Plus, I detest vulnerability. But when I finally attained the courage and began publicly sharing my writing on Instagram, I christened my writing with the pen name *cjLeubh*. I am a faithful believer of love and its powerful force, so I combined the old English term 'leubh' (love) with my initials, creating a façade and hiding from I don't know what. But today, I leave that behind, and I surrender my insecurities to you. My participation in the *Latinx Poetry Project* truly made me believe I can be who I want to be, and a poet is one of those things.

All she is will help you navigate the many parts of my being. As I have matured into the woman I am today, I have come to find I am everything I cannot see. I am strength, I am perseverance, I am feelings, I am words, I am thoughts, I am loneliness, I am heartbreak, I am two languages, but above all, I am *leubh*. With *All she is*, I am giving you all I have let go of, all I have gained, and all I aspire to be.

I am giving you *me*.

I am a poet.

Yours,
Cyn.

Acknowledgements

To Roxana, my love, my best friend, thank you for your unconditional love, support, and patience all through this process. Thank you for remaining my no. 1 fan since the days I would very timidly read you my poems when we were just teenagers. This project would not have been possible without you.

To Milo, mi cosa, for your faithful companionship and for not asking me to walk you in the middle of my writing workshops. I owe you.

To Angel Lem from LEMeKNOW Podcast for being the very first one to expose my work and insisting I'd write a book. I am in forever debt to you.

To the Alegria Magazine Team, you have changed my life. Special thanks to Davina Ferreira for opening me the doors to a whole new world.

To my family and friends, I wouldn't be here without your love and encouragement.

Finally, to my readers and all those who have been supportive of my art, you all have manifested this book into a reality.

desahogándome

(unburdening)

SENTIMENTS

love,
sometimes the only
and single reason needed
to go to hell and burn.

IRONÍA

perderla fue como morirse
de frío en un infierno.

PIECES OF YOU

i've been scattering pieces of you all over town –
words that some may call art
words of a broken heart that whisper into the air
unwritten poetry that only I can feel.

i never predicted the end.

VERSO I

vives en mi puño y letra.

THE MISCONCEPTION OF BLACK

black is poetic
and i love the darkness you left behind
in me.

and while i am searching for the *why*,
to the world, i give away the love you
wouldn't take from me.

i write.

VERSO II

enterré tu nombre en cada una de mis poesías.

ARTISTS believe in the nature of the broken to create a masterpiece of the unsaid.

VERSO III

el amor eterno es de papel,
y tú y yo no supimos escribirlo.

PRAYERS

ironically,
i begged the heavens for you to leave,
i asked him to take you away
if *He* thought you were no good for me.

and here i am,
waiting for your return.

padre nuestro que estás en el cielo...

HE KEEPS ME WARM

i sleep with the devil just to feel you closer.

VERSO IV

por las noches me convierto en luna,
velando tu recuerdo

I'LL BE THERE

and tonight,
before you close your eyes,
before you ease your mind
and feel with your heart,
in that genuine moment,

i hope
i wish

for that instant, you concede with the thought of me.

you know,
that space in between reality and
what-wasn't- meant- to-be,

i'll be there.

DULCE TORMENTO

te pienso.
te recuerdo.
te siento.
te sueño.
te lloro.
te escribo
y no te olvido.

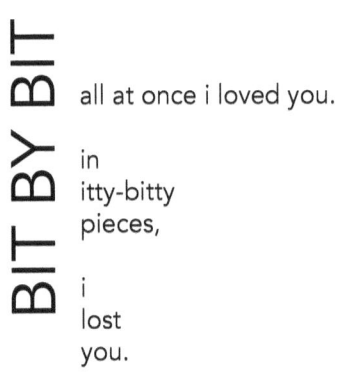

BIT BY BIT

all at once i loved you.

in
itty-bitty
pieces,

i
lost
you.

VERSO V

uno ama para estar vivo
y yo aquí, muriéndome.

ALL OF ME

i gave you everything,
even all that i wasn't.

SABIOS CONSEJOS

el corazón no siempre sabe lo que para él
es bueno pero como dijo Bukowski:

*descubre lo que verdaderamente amas
y deja que te mate.*

yo te encontré a ti.

KISMET

inevitably,
you and i belong together
but s e p a r a t e.

TÚ Y YO SOMOS UNO MISMO

tú allá
yo acá

tú con él
yo con ella

y, aún asi
no existe nadie entre los dos

COLD BREEZE

she was like the wind;
i couldn't see her,
but i could still feel her.

i am cold.

JUDAS

she was his Judas.

he would've forgiven her
but she never asked for forgiveness.

HOY, MAÑANA Y SIEMPRE

te quiero hoy tanto como ayer te amé
y como jamás podré querer mañana.

M.L.R.

and when i miss you the most,
i whisper your name.

VERSO VI

lo malo de que al morir de amor
aun sigues vivo.

SUNSHINE OF THE SPOTLESS MIND

i've forgotten everything about you,
except the way you made me feel.

VERSO VII

el alma se entrega sólo una vez.
el corazón, dos.

CAN'T LET GO

after you left,
my deepest fear wasn't that
you wouldn't come back

my deepest fear was facing the slightest possibility
of not loving again and then from that moment on
everyone would be no more than an empty companionship

did you find the note that i wrote?

VERSO VIII

la fidelidad no es cosa del cuerpo,
es cosa del alma.

A LIFETIME

i've only missed you once since the day you left, and i have not stopped ever since.

VERSO IX

el tiempo no sabe remendar ausencias
ni llenar vacíos.

REMEMBER ME ALWAYS

and if you ever think of me
don't neglect the thought

let it penetrate into the heart i once called mine
and let it rest in your soul for the times of need

i'll always be there,
if it is me that you need.

ps.
don't think of me
but remember me always

AYER siempre te voy a querer,
pero ya no te quiero.

en el corazón te llevaré
sin acordarme de ti.

MUTE my soul shouts "i miss you" whispers.

VERSO X

prefiero morir de amor y mendigarlo,
a morir con la duda y el alma seca.

FOREVER YOU & ME

i want to be the sweetest *nothing*,
you'll never forget.

the random thought,
you will never consider
and your most tormenting *what if*.

TONTA

te busco,
te busco,
y te busco,
pero tengo miedo a encontrarte.

lo que queremos no siempre es lo que necesitamos...

aquí te espero.

MIRADAS

you and i speak the unspoken word;
our most intimate conversations
have been from across the room.

VERSO XI

querer y no querer.
queriendo sin querer
y querer todo sin poder.

MARKED

yes, i wrote to you.

i wrote you for years,
until i ran out of words
and the thought of you
just became it – a thought.

a stain.

FRENESÍ

quiero,
quiero todo y nada.
quiero ser la verdad de todas tus mentiras.
quiero ser el amor de tu alma.
el peor error que hayas cometido,
pero que en silencio tanto glorificas.
quiero ser el peor recuerdo que jamás podrás olvidar.
quiero ser todo lo que quieres,
pero que no puedes tener.
quiero que trates de olvidarme
y que falles en cada intento.
quiero que me ames,
aunque sea en silencio.
quiero ser parte de tu ser
aun en la distancia.
quiero ser toda tuya,
quiero que seas toda mía sin que nos volvamos a ver.
tu en tu mundo,
yo en el mío
unidas por una maldición
que algunos inocentes podrían confundir con el amor
mientras que tu y yo le llamamos –

nuestro peor error.

DESAMOR

y cómo crees que se sienta el
amor después de ver su fracaso
entre tu y yo?

viviéndome
(living on)

RESURRECIÓN

me tocas y no te siento.
nuestra piel contra roza
y huelo a soledad.

tócame amor mío,
para sentirme tuya.

tócame amor mío,
para sentirme yo misma,
y acaríciame el alma
para sentirme viva.

BRUJERIA

one of our greatest possessions is touch.

MI SEGUNDA VIDA

yes, i loved you
and even called you *the love of my life*,
but you see,
i don't live that life anymore

HEALING

i've written myself out of love.

HAZAÑA HEROICA

falling in love is easy.
allowing someone to love you is the hard part.

vulnerability.

NO ERES TÚ, SOY YO

el *i love you* de cada mañana le dejaba un sabor desabrido en los labios.

LOVE IS A SKILL

everyone talks about the importance of
spreading love to the world.
but most forget that learning how to accept
love and allowing it in one's life
is just as important.

self-love is a skill not everyone can master.

VERSO XII

quiero volver a respirar en tu corazón
y ahogarme en tu piel.

GANAS DE TI

tengo ganas de ti.
respirar tu profundidad,
oler la esencia de tu alma,
probar de tu sed,
perderme en tu mirada,
revivir en tu libertad y
beber de tu piel.

tengo ganas de ti.
tengo ganas de descubrirte
para así llenarme de mi.

descubrir lo desconocido y
crear caminos

tengo ganas de ti
y de ser contigo.

LOVE ME TO PIECES

there are many ways to love a broken person;
common sense is not one of them.

love me until i am me again.

VERSO XIII

quiero conocer el secreto del futuro contigo.

TIME

it was in that particular moment;
when i first saw you,
that time came with the possibility
of an eternity.

you are my forever.

ALWAYS, ALWAYS & ALWAYS

love me forever
-she said

that, i cannot say my dear, for we all have different forevers designed by destiny.
i do, however, promise to love you always, always and always until the very last second of my forever's last breath.
-i replied

descubriéndome
(uncovering)

SIN NADIE MÁS

since we begin to reason life teaches us about
broken love *busca tu otra mitad* – they say

only teaching us that we are broken and not whole
and desperately we yearn for that 'missing piece'.

as an adult now, i question the ideology.
i have come to learn i am whole
i now understand my value as an individual
and i am in no need of 'mi otra mitad'

soy única
soy fuerte
soy independiente

soy mi abuela
soy mi madre

soy cada ser que he vivido
también soy mucho mi padre

pero al final –
soy yo.

i need you whole,
not your half.
soy tuya y soy de mi
sin nadie más.

REFLEXIONANDO

before you there was me.
if there is ever an after you,
there will still be me.

so, i don't need you.
i need us.

('i need you' – words i never used again)

I AM A WOMAN

i am a woman
but i have never been a girl
i've always been a boy

i was born to win
i was born to lead

call me crazy
call me naïve
call me lesbian
call me feminist
call me anything you want

but don't call me weak
i belong with the pack

i am a woman
and i was born to lead

36-24-36

her body was only an outer shell.
a rather limited and distorted
perception of a deeper reality.

she is more.

MANIFESTACIONES

soy pagina 40
pagina 41
soy la duda y el miedo en mi voz
temblorosa
puño fuerte y liberador
esperanza del triunfo
corazón mudo y delirante
inspirante.

soy libertad
liberación

soy pagina 40
pagina 41

si puedo
soy talento
soy poesía

poeta

CREO

creo en Dios,
pero no leo la Biblia.

creo en la felicidad,
pero no en la perfección.

creo en el amor,
pero no en el cuento de hadas.

creo en el 'más allá',
pero sé que el 'más allá' se encuentra más acá.

creo en el hoy y el mañana,
pero sé que sin el ayer no seríamos nadie.

creo en los errores,
pero no los confundamos con un estilo de vida.

creo en la verdad,
pero sé que no existe sin la mentira.

creo en mis miedos,
sólo me nutren de valentía.

creo en la eternidad instante,
pero no en un 'por siempre'.

creo que no hay sentimiento más puro que el de un corazón roto,
te hace sentir débil y vivo a la vez.

creo saber todo,
y sé que no sé nada.

creo,
lo sé.

BECOMING

i am dying,
every day that i live, i am dying.

i've shed and renewed my skin time after time again.
i am continuously reconstructing myself and evolving,
always becoming someone new.

i do not know who i'll be next.
i'll probably be more centered and less stressed.

nevertheless,
all i want to be is happy.
leave every sad part of me behind
without forgetting the path i've walked,
without forgetting those who i have lived,
without forgetting every lesson learned.

i am dying,
and all i want is to be happy.

i am everything i cannot see.
i know there is more to me.

i am dying,
every day that i live
i am dying,

every day that i live,
i am becoming.

ME

i've been silent,
i've been quiet,
i've let the outside roar make its noise
and i've said nothing.

i've been confused,
yet as happy as i can be.

i found meaning in life once again
just as the world began falling apart.

i don't understand.

they are trying to condemn us and restrain us from freedom
i represent all that they oppose, and i can't help but wonder
if i will be next.

i am an educated, queer, mexican american woman.
someone who represents an undesirable threat to their
conservative moral views and values.
someone who is much worse than the rapist priest, whom
they have invited into their home.
someone who is much worse than the mass murders of
innocent people our wars create, in the name of our *patria*.
i am more of a threat than the pedophile they've shared
christmas and family dinners with.

i am a threat because i am free.
free to exist.

why do they insist to label me as _____?
why should i label myself in order to be considered
or feel like i belong?

why should i label as gay/ lesbian/ or queer?
why should i label myself as anything other than human,
si el *Dios de los cielos ya me dio permiso?*

i am human.

there is no gender,
there is no race,
no religion,
they are all man- made to keep us tamed.

life just is
and so it should be

do not label me so your ignorant society can keep suppressing
all those who are different, unique and free.

i am me.

LA VIDA MISMA

y si me preguntaras,
¿qué quieres ser en la vida?

te diría:

quiero ser luz. quiero ser fuego. quiero ser amor.

quiero ser amor del que duele. amor que amarra. amor que sofoca. amor que te teje del hilo del corazón un suéter. amor demente. amor que te enciende. amor en la intimidad. amor en el sexo. amor abstinente. amor que miente. amor que protege. amor que inspira. amor que causa rabia. amor que atormenta. amor que mata. amor que engrandece. amor que alimenta. amor que nunca se olvida. amor instantáneo. amor honesto. amor eterno. amor fugaz. un amor inexplicable. amor no provocado. amor admirable. amor de libreto. amor en una palabra. amor en papel. amor en un nombre. amor sin palabras. amor que hiere. amor tierno. amor frágil. amor puro. amor incondicional. amor sonriente. amor apasionado. amor en nada. amor en todo. amor en silencio. amor a gritos. amor en un roce. amor en un beso. amor en un suspiro. amor en el vientre. amor en la mente. amor en los labios. amor en el corazón. amor en la piel. amor de día. amor de noche. amor de madrugada. amor en soledad. amor en los libros. amor en las estrellas. amor en las botellas. amor en un sueño. amor en la realidad. amor al despertar. amor al amanecer. amor en un café. amor en la puesta del sol. amor al anochecer. amor en la naturaleza. amor en el arte. amor en un abrazo. un amor inesperado. amor en tus manos. amor en tus ojos. amor en el subconsciente. amor inocente. amor obsesionado. amor seductivo. amor con experiencia. amor no correspondido. amor primero. amor anhelado. amor lejano. amor distante. amor al costado. amor sin contratos. amor sin despedida. amor liberal. amor que no sabe decir adiós. amor a la antigua. amor en el memento mori.

y si me preguntaras,
¿qué quieres ser en la vida?
te diría:

la vida misma.

NEGRA

negra,
negrita,
prietita,
sandillita.

¡ay que piel tan mas bonita!

piel color tierra,
color canela,
color campo,
color historia,
color cultura.

you see,
i was raised at *calle chapultepec* #112, or *la turquía*, o
la calle de las brujas as it was best known by the locals,
but to me, #112 has always been my safe heaven – my
Papa Nacho's and *Mama Lupe's* house in Michoacán for
four years, el #112 *fue una casa con mucho ruido, amor,
humildad,* consejos y una que otra travesura.

negra
negrita
prietita
sandillita

¡ay que piel tan mas bonita!

mi barbie negrita,
decía mi tía Berta, hermana de mi Papa Nacho

apodos que conocí
y abrasé con amor, orgullo y dulzura.

i now know racism in mexico exists -
negra!,
prieta!
india/o pata rajada!
insinuaciones deplorables de la boca del mexicano.

i now know racism exists,
shit, it's all over the media!

but *negra, negrita*
en mi mundo de niña habían sido palabras muy bonitas
and it was not until i retuned 'to the land of the free'
that i learned the term *negra/o* was offensive and oppressive.
it was an insult
y ahora eran palabras que dolían
palabras que marchitan el alma
e insultan toda una cultura,
e ignoran toda una historia

so much pain –

tanto dolor,
tanta tortura
tanta impotencia

pero como les explico que
negra
negrita
han sido para mi, palabras muy llenas de amor

negra
negrita
la llevo en el alma

negra
negrita,
palabras, apodos, nombres que me hacen ser,
y que, de vez en vez, Cynthia ya no quiero ser.

LUGAR CERCA DEL CIELO

if i could time-travel
i'd always go home.

i would travel hacia mi infancia.
a la tierra que me vió crecer.
tierra que me regaló una niñez muy feliz.
donde aprendí el valor de las cosas simples
y sobre la humildad.
donde aprendí a correr libremente con los carrizos y sin zapatos.
donde aprendí la hermandad y complicidad entre primos.

i would go home.
donde el olor a tierra mojada trae vida.
donde la sequía o el canalito de agua se convertían en el parque acuático más divertido.

donde jugábamos a las escondidas, a las traes, a la patadita, a la lotería, al palito, al fútbol, a brincar la reata o a contar leyendas del pueblo muy antiguas.

i would go home.
donde la puesta de sol anuncia paz y el fin de una larga jornada.

donde mi abuela, Mamá Lupe
me enseñó a tortear y a mezclar el nixtamal
y nos regalaba su amor en cada "ranita" de masa con sal,
bien calientita.

i would go home.
donde mi abuelo, Papá Nacho
nos regaló su legado con su tierra que ahora lleva por nombre "Pedregal San Ignacio".

i would always go home.
donde mis padres soñaron juntos
con un mejor futuro y su casa de dos pisos

i would go home.
donde los mayos son muy calientes
pero se respira una fresca fé todo el mes.
porque en mayo se venera la llegada del Santo Cristo Milagroso; el patrón, el todopoderoso
mayo es cuando hay peregrinaciones, mandas, sacrificios, gente del norte, reuniones
familiares, cenadurías, música, bailes, la rueda de la fortuna, el castillo pirotécnico, citas de amor en el quiosco y confetti, mucho confetti.

i would go home
to Tanhuato, Michoacán -
"lugar cerca del cerro", en Chichimeca.

i would always go home
to Tanhuato, Michoacán -
"lugar cerca del cielo", en mi propia lengua.

BURDEN

men
men

i carry their weight
i carry their weight on my shoulders
i carry their weight on my back
i carry their weight on my soul

men
i carry their names dry on my lips

men
men
i have loved them like they haven't loved me
i love them empty
i love them full
and in between

men
i have loved them unconditionally

men
men
can you see me?

men
men
can you feel me?

men
men
can you hear me?

men
men
do you even fucking care?

PENSAMIENTOS TORMENTOSOS

i am angry
i am mad
and i don't know why

could it be my easily triggered stress?
the often pressure of reaching nothing less than perfection?
or the anguishing thought of feeling like life owes me something?
or could it just be that fact that he too disappeared after mom died?

i am angry
i am mad
¡y quiero gritar!

could it be all the pain i suppressed after mom's death?
could it be because i am gay but somehow it is still a secret?

do i hold resentment and i am not aware?
could it because he never offered to pay for my school, and i had to work for it instead?
could it be the fact that life hasn't been easy and at times extremely lonely even when in company?

or could it be because at 14 i had to grow up and become a wife, mom, sister, daughter and still be a teenager while questioning my sexual identity?

or could it be because my older brother struggles with alcohol abuse and depression
and i don't know how to handle it?

or could it be the fact that my relationship with my
youngest brother is hanging by a thread
and i refuse to lose him, but i don't know how to
handle it?

or can my resentment be because the first time i
loved, love broke my existence into pieces
and i didn't know how to handle it?

i am a good woman
i have a good soul
why doesn't dad care to be part of my life?

he has pushed me to build my own family
with people i feel safe
but have very little common with
he wasn't brave enough to keep the four of us
together.

i am angry

but i know how to hold my broken pieces together.
i have learned to be my own keeper.

¡quiero gritar!

solo escribo.

OVERACHIEVER

i've witnessed the power of a prayer.
i've witnessed destiny work its course.
i've been blessed beyond possibilities
and yet,
i've doubted my abilities
i've doubted my blessings
i've doubted my destiny
even when the universe has manifested itself
before me time and time again,
assuring me i was born to shine.

i am an overthinker;
~~it is a curse.~~
it is a gift.
it is my art.

i've made it this far.

YOU CHOOSE

they say:
"what doesn't kill you makes you stronger"

i say:
nonsense.

it does kill you.
it kills you softly
and it completely changes you.

you become stronger
but it is not a strength
because with time you discover you now feel a little less

you now feel numb.

and that could either be a blessing or a curse.

a blessing or a curse?

a blessing
or
a
curse?

NO HAY PEOR CIEGO QUE EL QUE NO QUIERE VER

me enoje con la vida
y con toda la rabia me olvide de ella
hasta que deje de sentir

me quitó tanto que la aborrecí
y con el corazón entumido
seguí mi camino

deje de ver lo bueno que me ofrecía
y me aferre a la amargura que a diario inhalaba

mi pensar ingenuo e inmaduro no me permitía
ver la realidad –
había logrado tanto,
y aun así me sentía vacía

nada llenaba las dudas del pasado

porque a mi!? – preguntaba
porque a mi!? – exclamaba

ahora,
ya puedo cerrar los ojos y ver con claridad –

en la vida se pierde y se gana
se gana y se pierde
se gana y se gana
se pierde y se pierde

a mi me toco perder para ganar

dolió.
pero hoy sigo ganando.

es la realidad.

DAYDREAMING

despierto,
lo primero que hago es coger el teléfono y le llamo a mamá
le pregunto si nos podemos ver el fin de semana
que la extraño mucho y quiero apapacharla
también le digo que se me antojan sus ricas enchiladas

le pregunto por el Viejo
me dice que ha estado trabajando mucho
pero que dentro de un mes le promete un viaje a Michoacán
se escucha muy emocionada

me siento completa

después de una corta charla,
le digo que me tengo que ir,
que me espera un día muy largo en el juzgado
y tengo que prepararme

antes de colgar me da su bendición
y me dice el cuán orgullosa de mi se siente

me siento completa

haciéndoseme ya tarde,
antes de salir por la puerta
Mario, mi hermano mayor, me manda un mensaje diciendo

que me tiene una sorpresa
y Gilberto, el menor, me dice que me invita a
cenar está noche, que tiene algo muy importante
que compartir conmigo

me siento completa

ya voy tarde
azoto la puerta detrás de mi
y aún así me detengo
cierro los ojos y suspiro profundo

siento un dolor en el pecho

acabo de describir la vida que nunca viví

Mamá murió
el Viejo se enamoró
Mario se distanció
y Gilberto olvidó

estoy incompleta

MY MISSING VOICE

i close my eyes
and something within me awakes the memory of you.

i imagine your smile,
and i smile.

my being resonates with the warm thought of you
and i sigh.

my heart begins to rapidly palpitate in melancholia and despair,
yet somehow, i feel complete.

i pause.

i unconsciously ask:
what if?

i quietly whisper:
i know we would've been the best of friends

i imagine your smile
and i smile.

i'd like you to know there is always a sigh after each happy moment
in hope of filling the empty space in my chest.

i am awake.
you are my missing voice.

en donde quiera que estés,
i miss you Mother.

ÁNGEL DE MI GUARDA

te vi.

te vi en toda tu esencia
vivias en mi presente
y yo en tu infinidad.

for a moment,
i was somebody's daughter.

solo fue un sueño.

MOTHERS AND DAUGHTERS

i am never going to have that –

i will never know what you were made of,
much less what made you be.

i will never know your story,
i will never know the woman –
only what i lived as a kid.

sometimes,
or perhaps more often than i wished,
i feel deeply the thought of you
and it hurts.

it hurts to feel like i wasn't there for you.
i was much too afraid to deal with the thought of losing you
that i hopelessly believed God wouldn't betray my faith.
i was only 14 – he wouldn't do something like that to me.

i didn't know.

but even when in doubt, i would pray and hope you'd heal.

it didn't work.

once, i had a dream.
you had come back,
it was all a medical misunderstanding and you were only
asleep all this time.

for many years, i wished this were true.

since your departure,
i've been afraid of risking my heart.
afraid of loving so deeply and being torn apart.

but i remain hopeful.

i know when the time comes,
and i find myself living the life i was destined,
when the time comes and i see my love reflected in my own child's eyes,
i know she will teach me what you were made of and what made you be.

her name will be your name
so that when mine dissolves into "mom",
yours will come to life again
and every time i call her; Lou,
i will remember every little thing about you.

i will never have that –
i will never know first-hand what you were made of
or what made you be,
but i will have you both.

About the author

Cynthia J. Villa is a queer, Mexican American poet, and writer from Wilmington, California. As a child, she lived in Michoacán, Mexico, with her parents and two brothers. Upon her troubling return to *el Norte* and her struggles with the cultural clash, she eventually learned to exist in-between two languages. Yearning to alleviate the grief, heartache, and ambiguity caused by her mother's unpredictable death became the pivotal point that invited her to submerge in the mythical world of poetry. Eventually, her writings became a proclamation of self-healing. Her poetry now immerses in themes of Love, Loss, Heartache, Healing, and Self-Empowerment. She has exhibited her work under the pen name, *cjLeubh*, on social platforms. Some of her most recent work was featured in Alegria Magazine's, *The Latinx Poetry Project*. As a primary witness of the effects of the struggles of cultural and language barriers and the lack of resources and representation of people of color in low-income communities, she's been inspired to pursue a legal career. Whether it is in immigration law or criminal law, she aspires to become a lawyer not to punish people but to ensure the law protects the people it is meant to protect. When Cynthia is not writing or spending time with her partner and their dog Milo, you'll find her wandering in the isles of Ikea or HomeGoods.

To connect with Cynthia:
email cjvillapoetry@gmail.com
Instagram @cjvilla_

www.ingramcontent.com/pod-product-compliance
Lightning Source LLC
Chambersburg PA
CBHW031128080526
44587CB00011B/1154